What's in this book

This book belongs to

_____

我喜欢水果 I like fruit

学习内容 Contents

沟通 Communication

说说喜欢吃什么、喝什么
Talk about what someone likes to eat and drink

问他人喜欢吃什么、喝什么
Ask about what someone likes to eat and drink

生词 New words

★ 喜欢　to like

★ 吃　to eat

★ 水果　fruit

★ 喝　to drink

★ 果汁　fruit juice

★ 水　water

★ 不　not, no

苹果　apple

香蕉　banana

葡萄　grape

我喜欢（喝）果汁。

I like fruit juice.

我喜欢（吃）苹果。

I like apples.

你喜欢吃什么？

What do you like to eat?

你喜欢喝什么？

What do you like to drink?

文化 Cultures

中国特产水果——荔枝

Chinese speciality fruit — lychee

跨学科学习 Project

统计哪种水果受欢迎，
画出图表

Conduct a survey on fruit
and make a pictogram

Get ready

1 What is your favourite fruit?

2 Do you eat fruit every day?

3 What fruit do you think Brownie likes?

chī
吃

shuǐ guǒ
水果

我喜欢吃水果。

妈妈喜欢苹果，爸爸喜欢香蕉。

hē
喝

guǒ zhī
果汁

shuǐ
水

姐姐喜欢喝果汁。

布朗尼，你喜欢吃什么？

小心！小狗不能吃葡萄。

你不能吃葡萄，我也不
吃了。

Let's think

1 What do they like? Match the pictures to the people.

2 Why can't Brownie eat grapes? Discuss with your friend.

小心！小狗不能吃葡萄。

New words

1 Learn the new words.

喜欢　苹果　水　不　吃　水果　葡萄　喝　香蕉　果汁

2 Match the words to the pictures.
Write the letters.

a 吃　　b 喝　　c 水果
d 不喜欢　　e 喜欢

1 Listen and decide. Put a tick or a cross.

 2 Look at the pictures. Listen to the sto

1

2

3

4

d say.

Complete the sentences and say.

1

我们喜欢吃……

2

这是我的……

3

那是姐姐的……

4

你……吃什么水果？

13

Task

Count and write the number of fruit on each plate. Tell your friend.

苹果：_____

苹果：_____

葡萄：_____

香蕉：_____

Game

Play a relay game.

这是什么水果？

这是香蕉。我喜欢吃香蕉。这是什么水果？

这是……我喜欢吃……这是什么水果？

……

Song

🎧 05 Listen and sing.

喜欢吃水果吗？

苹果、香蕉和葡萄，

你喜欢吃什么？

喜欢喝果汁吗？

苹果汁、葡萄汁，

你喜欢喝什么？

课堂用语 Classroom language

拿出铅笔。
Take out a pencil.

拿出橡皮。
Take out a rubber.

学中文。
Learn Chinese.

写一写 Write

1 Learn and trace the stroke.

提

2 Learn the component. Trace 氵 in the characters.

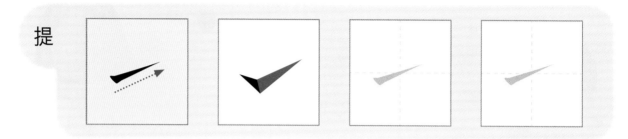

氵 浩 汁 没 洗

3 Circle the characters with 氵.

河　凉
点　燕　渠
浩　冰　海
热　照
汉　冷

4 Trace and write the character.

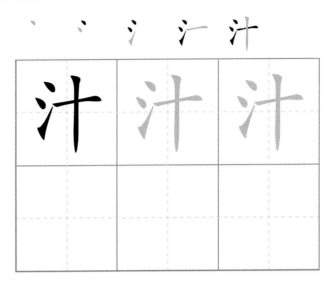

Over 3,000 years ago, Chinese characters were carved on bones. They looked like pictures.

Learn how the character for *water* has changed into the character we see today.

Can you guess the meaning of the character below?

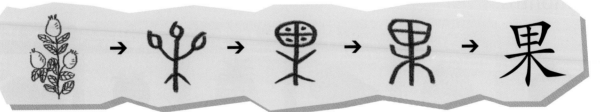

Follow the instructions.

Look	Draw	Write

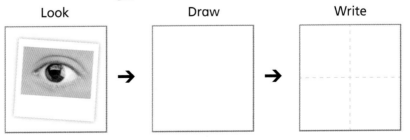

Cultures

1 Have you seen this fruit before?

This is a lychee, a summer fruit with a sweet flavour. It is grown in Southern China and has a history of over 2,000 years.

2 Find your favourite fruit and tell your friend the harvest months.

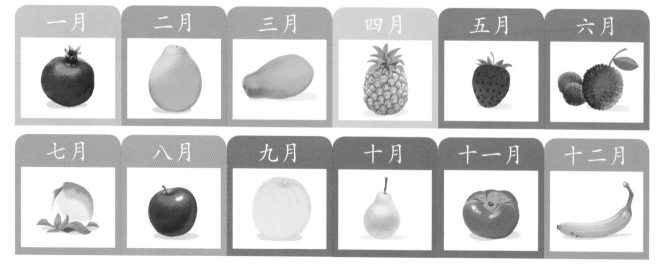

1 What fruit is popular in your class? Write the numbers and say.

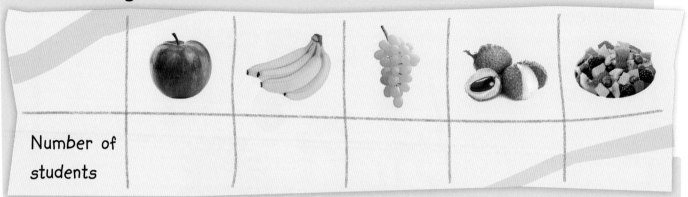

Number of students					

2 Colour the fruit survey pictogram. Discuss with your friend.

＿＿＿＿个人
喜欢吃葡萄。

＿＿＿＿个人
喜欢吃苹果。

1 Play the board game by starting from the bottom. Answer in Chinese.

Tell the Monkey King:

我 ⋯⋯ 吃 ⋯⋯

Finish

Circle the component for 'water'.

浩浩

河

Write the character.

果

你喜欢喝水吗？

这是什么？

这是什么？

这是什么？

这是什么？

这是什么？

Start

2 Work with your friend. Colour the stars and the chillies.

Words	说	读	写
喜欢	☆	☆	🌶
吃	☆	☆	🌶
水果	☆	☆	🌶
喝	☆	☆	🌶
果汁	☆	☆	🌶
水	☆	☆	🌶
不	☆	☆	🌶
苹果	☆	🌶	🌶
香蕉	☆	🌶	🌶
葡萄	☆	🌶	🌶

Sentences	说	读	写
我喜欢 (吃) 苹果。	☆	🌶	🌶
我喜欢 (喝) 果汁。	☆	☆	🌶
你喜欢吃什么？	☆	☆	🌶
你喜欢喝什么？	☆	☆	🌶

Talk about what someone likes eating and drinking	☆
Ask about what someone likes eating and drinking	☆

3 What does your teacher say?

My teacher says ...

分享 Sharing

Words I remember

喜欢	xǐ huan	to like
吃	chī	to eat
水果	shuǐ guǒ	fruit
喝	hē	to drink
果汁	guǒ zhī	fruit juice
水	shuǐ	water
不	bù	not, no
苹果	píng guǒ	apple
香蕉	xiāng jiāo	banana
葡萄	pú tao	grape

Other words

布朗尼	bù lǎng ní	Brownie, name of a dog
小心	xiǎo xīn	be careful
小狗	xiǎo gǒu	puppy
能	néng	can
也	yě	also, too
荔枝	lì zhī	lychee

OXFORD
UNIVERSITY PRESS

Oxford University Press is a department of the University of Oxford.
It furthers the University's objective of excellence in research, scholarship,
and education by publishing worldwide. Oxford is a registered trade mark of
Oxford University Press in the UK and in certain other countries

Published in Hong Kong by
Oxford University Press (China) Limited
39th Floor, One Kowloon, 1 Wang Yuen Street, Kowloon Bay,
Hong Kong

Illustrated by Anne Lee and Wildman

Photographs for reproduction permitted by Dreamstime.com

China National Publications Import & Export (Group) Corporation is an authorized distributor of
Oxford Elementary Chinese.

Please contact content@cnpiec.com.cn or 86-10-65856782

ISBN: 978-0-19-082142-5

10 9 8 7 6 5 4 3 2